# Living Treasures

By Mary Lindeen

**Scott Foresman**
is an imprint of

Glenview, Illinois • Boston, Massachusetts • Chandler, Arizona
Upper Saddle River, New Jersey

**Photographs**

Every effort has been made to secure permission and provide appropriate credit for photographic material. The publisher deeply regrets any omission and pledges to correct errors called to its attention in subsequent editions.

Unless otherwise acknowledged, all photographs are the property of Pearson Education, Inc.

Photo locators denoted as follows: Top (T), Center (C), Bottom (B), Left (L), Right (R), Background (Bkgd)

**CVR** PhotoLibrary Group, Ltd.; **1** Dex Image/Jupiter Images; **3** AP Images/©AP Photo; **4** Dex Image/Jupiter Images; **5** © Jack Fields/Corbis; **6** © Jack Fieldsca/Corbis; **7** AP Images/©AP Photo; **8** © Photo Resource Hawaii/Alamy Images; **9** Michael Goldman/ Getty Images; **10** © Jim West /Alamy Images; **11** Rubberball/Jupiter Images; **12** Jupiter Images; **13** © Jim West /Alamy Images; **14** © Randy Eli Grothe/Dallas Morning News/ Corbis, © Marc Brasz//Corbis, Ramin Talaie/Corbis; **15** ©Todd Wright/Getty Images; **16** PhotoLibrary Group, Ltd.

ISBN 13: 978-0-328-47292-5
ISBN 10:      0-328-47292-1

**Copyright © by Pearson Education, Inc., or its affiliates.** All rights reserved. Printed in the United States of America. This publication is protected by copyright, and permission should be obtained from the publisher prior to any prohibited reproduction, storage in a retrieval system, or transmission in any form or by any means, electronic, mechanical, photocopying, recording, or likewise. For information regarding permissions, write to Pearson Curriculum Rights & Permissions, One Lake Street, Upper Saddle River, New Jersey 07458.

**Pearson®** is a trademark, in the U.S. and/or in other countries, of Pearson plc or its affiliates.
**Scott Foresman®** is a trademark, in the U.S. and/or in other countries, of Pearson Education, Inc., or its affiliates.

3 4 5 6 7 8 9 10 V010 13 12 11 10

In Japan, the third Monday of September is Respect for the Aged Day. This national holiday celebrates senior citizens.

All over Japan, people honor the long lives and wisdom of their elders. They make special meals, hold special events, and give gifts to senior citizens.

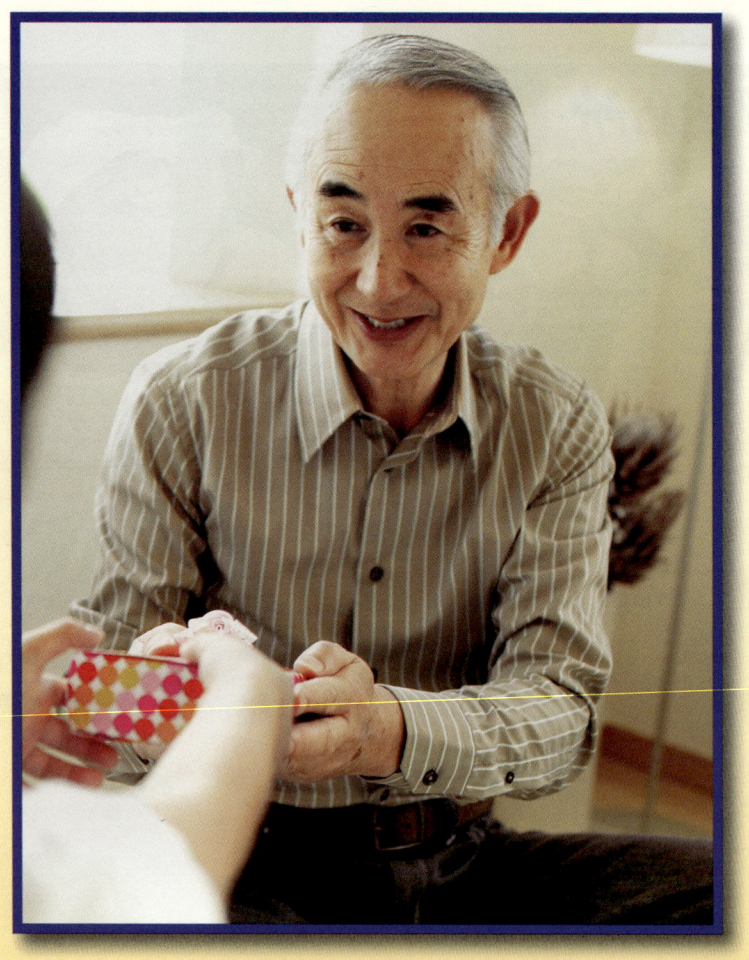

Japan also honors its Living National Treasures. These are senior citizens who have made important contributions to Japanese life and culture.

Some Living National Treasures have spent their lives studying ancient Japanese arts, such as making kimonos, weaving bamboo, or working a *Bunraku* puppet.

Other countries also celebrate the wisdom and skill of older people. They recognize that senior citizens have a lifetime of learning and information to share.

Many older people have made it their job to keep ancient traditions alive in art, dance, or music. They have a lot to teach and show us about cultural practices from long ago.

Senior citizens can tell amazing stories from their younger days. What was it like to live on a submarine in World War II? How did they get up every morning in the dark to milk the cows on their farm? What did they do before color TV, computers, and cell phones? Even just 50 years ago, everyday life was very different.

Some older people volunteer in their community after they retire. Another pair of helping hands is always needed in schools, hospitals, and parks.

Instead of retiring, many senior citizens choose to keep right on working. They can be an important resource in the workplace, sharing what they know and offering ways to solve problems.

Others give their time in another way. They help their families. Many grandparents or older family members take care of young children in the family. This gives parents a little extra free time. It gives children another person who loves, cares, and watches out for them.

Many older people are no longer raising a family or working full-time. Instead, they travel wherever help is needed. They might go to a city hit by floods or hurricanes. They might travel to another country to share their knowledge with farmers, nurses, or teachers.

A few senior citizens become very well known for their talents and contributions. But most go more quietly about their lives, simply sharing their wisdom, skills, and time.

14

Growing old isn't always easy or fun, and no one knows that better than senior citizens themselves. But with age—and a lifetime of experiences—comes wisdom.

Do you know a senior citizen who is important in your life? Think about all you can learn from and share with this person. Don't overlook the Living Treasures in your family and your neighborhood!